BUDGETING
IS MORE LIBERATION
THAN LIMITATION

ROSHAWNNA NOVELLUS AND
ROOSEVELT J. SCALES

Budgeting Is More Liberation Than Limitation
Copyright © 2015 Novellus Financial

All Rights Reserved. Published 2015. No part of this publication may be reproduced, distributed, or transmitted in any form or by any means, including photocopying, recording, or other electronic or mechanical methods, without the prior written permission of the publisher, except in the case of brief quotations embodied in critical reviews and certain other noncommercial uses permitted by copyright law. For permission requests, write to the publisher, addressed "Attention: Permissions Coordinator," at the address below.

First published by Novellus Financial

ISBN 978-1-939761-36-1

Printed in the United States of America
Novellus Financial
931 Monroe Dr., Suite 102 #223
Atlanta, GA 30308
www.novellusfinancial.com

The contents of this book are for educational purposes and nothing contained herein should be construed as financial advice. The information provided in this book is not a complete analysis of every material fact for all individuals. Opinions expressed are subject to change without notice. Statements of fact cited have been obtained from sources considered reliable. No representation, however, is made as to the completeness or accuracy of any statement or numerical data.

This publication may include technical or other inaccuracies or typographical errors. Author assumes no responsibility for errors or omissions in this publication or other documents referenced by or linked to this publication or the related website.

Budgeting and financial planning require in-depth review of all areas of a person's life and finances in order to provide appropriate advice. Such analysis and review are not possible in a book format, but the principles herein are believed to be foundational in nature and are a starting point for gaining knowledge about budgeting.

Readers are encouraged to seek financial advice from competent professionals in the financial planning, investment advisory, legal, and insurance arenas so that the specific details of their situations can be considered as a whole. This publication is provided "as is" without warranty of any kind, either express or implied, including, but not limited to, the implied warranties of merchantability and fitness for a particular purpose or non-infringement.

In no event shall authors be liable for any damages whatsoever, including without limitation, special, incidental, indirect, or consequential damages of any kind, whether or not advised of the possibility of damage, and on any theory of liability, arising out of or in connection with the use of information in this publication.

Nothing contained herein is, in any way, a guarantee or assurance that following strategies outlined in this book will create financial success or security, and readers should understand that they are responsible for the actions they take or do not take as a result of reading this book.

CONTENTS

Acknowledgments..1
Epigraph...3
Our Principle Foundation...5

Part One: To Know, Not Guess...9
    Chapter 1: Resource Discovery...................................13
    Chapter 2: Gathering Experience................................23
    Chapter 3: From Data to Knowledge..........................33

Part Two: To Plan, Not Hope...41
    Chapter 4: Shifting Your Perception............................43
    Chapter 5: Hands-On Budget Planning......................51
    Chapter 6: Wise Habits..75

Part Three: To Liberate, Not Limit..................................81
    Chapter 7: Every Dollar Matters..................................83
    Chapter 8: Continue to Conquer.................................89

Thank You..91
About the Authors...92
What's Next?...96
Resources..97

ACKNOWLEDGEMENTS

Throughout my life, there have been individuals who have supported me wholeheartedly without expectation. You are true examples of Metta: Joyce, Gail, Duane, Yvonne, and Carver.
~ Roshawnna

One plants, another waters, and God gives the increase. Thank you to all who have influenced my path and my growth, especially Mommy, Pops, Sad, Tops, J, Elle, Dellie, Q, Isaac, and Henock.
~ Roosevelt

EPIGRAPH

"The aim is to cultivate your ability to plan your life around your resources to achieve your goals." – R. Scales

OUR PRINCIPLE FOUNDATION: TO LIBERATE, NOT LIMIT

If you're like most people, you spend a large portion of your life working. You exchange time and expertise for the opportunity to lead the life you desire. However, simply working and receiving an income is generally not sufficient to create your ideal life: true liberation.

Accomplishing true liberation requires disciplined planning, integrated with your finances and lifestyle.

Using a budget to direct your lifestyle is imperative because planning, wise decision-making, and discipline don't develop naturally; they must be cultivated.

The budgeting process is the framework used to convert opportunities into successes through planning. Therefore, budgeting is the essential outline in the path to financial liberation.

The overarching financial goal is to spend less than what you earn, using the excess to reduce debt, save, and invest. This concept is simple to grasp but difficult to accomplish; it takes discipline. Budgeting, like discipline, isn't about denying yourself, but being able to do and have what you want and accomplish your goals without fear, uncertainty, or limitations.

Eating balanced meals takes effort. Exercising takes effort. Aligning your life with your budget also takes effort. Achieving any goal requires the proper balance of input and output. You know the basic requirements of health, both financial and physical, but without a roadmap it is easy to veer off the path.

Think of budgeting as your roadmap; your guide to reaching your desired destination of financial liberation.

> **A budget is a financial planning process based on estimates of income and expenditures for a set period of time.**

If you are seeking financial freedom to do and have what you want in life, this book is for you. You might have tried other ways to accomplish your goals only to realize you have no plan and few finances to help you accomplish your dreams. By learning the basic process of budgeting and how it can help liberate you from lack, fear, and uncertainty, you will discover that you truly can accomplish all that you dream of.

Previous generations were happy with getting a job at a stable company and working there for 20+ years. However, the Millennials who make up the workforce of today could have as many as 15 to 20 jobs over the course of their working lives, according to the Future Workplace "Multiple Generations @ Work" survey. In fact, data published by the Bureau of Labor Statistics in 2012 reveals that people between the ages of 25 and 34 stayed at their current jobs for only 3.2 years on average. Therefore, the "new normal" for younger professionals is to live first, and work to support an ideal lifestyle. No matter what you want, you can make it happen by incorporating into your lifestyle the discipline of a budget.

My concept of freedom is a happy life achieved through proper diet, fitness, loving relationships, enriching travel, helping people, and running a successful business. Each of these components is integrated into my life to provide a sense of purpose, love, achievement, and contentment.

Budgeting, throughout my life, has enabled me to craft the freedom I have now. For example, I recently took a break from my work life to travel to Thailand for a yoga retreat. In the past, I've attended conferences for various intellectual pursuits, such as tax law and algorithm development, as well as traveled around the world via ship for four months to learn about various cultures and my true self. I have even moved to a new city without external employment.

I believe you can benefit from my experiences and practices demonstrated in this book. I hope this teaches and inspires you to achieve financial freedom.

You too have your vision of an ideal life. This book is designed to aid in the achievement of your financial liberation, as defined by you.

Proper financial preparation doesn't require an advanced financial education or specialized classes. The information shared in this book isn't difficult to digest, but is paramount in achieving financial freedom. Every step takes you closer to your ultimate goal.

To understand what financial freedom means to you, ask yourself:
- What do I want out of life?
- What is my ideal physical environment?
- What is my concept of a balanced life?
- What are my life priorities?
- How much money will I need to live my ideal life?
- How and how soon can I get there?

Your finances should reflect your life goals. These goals may include living in a certain city, having specific tangible items, enjoying certain experiences, learning, achieving career titles or designations, making a specific income, or attaining other elements that define freedom and your ideal lifestyle. Budgeting is your path to financial liberation.

 Budgeting does not add limits; it removes them.

Use this book, and the budgeting insight it gives you, to be the master of your destiny. Consider your financial goals, visualize your ideal lifestyle, plan for it, and take action to experience it.

Good luck, and happy reading!

Sincerely,

Roshawnna Novellus

PART ONE: TO KNOW, NOT GUESS

*"The eye sees only what the
mind is prepared to comprehend."
– Robertson Davies*

The first step to financial liberation is knowledge. According to a 2014 report by the Corporation for Enterprise Development (CFED), nearly half of the American population is "liquid asset poor," meaning they have less than three months worth of savings. In addition, a June 2014 Bankrate survey reported that 26 percent of Americans have no emergency savings.

Why is this important? Because having money on hand (liquid assets) is critical for managing life's little emergencies, including paying bills following a job loss, as well as covering the cost of unexpected repairs, funding health care expenses, and taking a vacation, among other things.

Many people, when asked to assess their current financial position, generally are uninformed, assess their position as subpar, or admit that they could benefit from financial education.

Unfortunately, many people do not take the necessary steps to do what they can to improve their financial situation. Can you relate to this? If so, it's time you take steps towards financial liberation and start living the life you've been dreaming about.

Financial liberation is achieved not only through income accumulation, but by also practicing expense reduction and debt elimination.

If you do not know your current financial position, it is impossible for you to live your ideal lifestyle or to properly plan your future, regardless of your economic status. Therefore, you must understand your current financial position.

When clients come to me for help with achieving their dreams, I ask them to tell me their net disposable income, which is defined as the difference between their income and their expenses. Often, clients guess at this figure. I also ask them to write down their income after taxes and expenses to verify that their net income is correct. As you can imagine, most of the time, their actual figure is much lower than what they initially guessed.

Net Disposable Income = Income - Expenses

Here is the problem. Say Vivica (not her real name) wanted to save $5,000 to take off of work for six weeks and spend time traveling to South America. She thinks she could save $500 per month for 10 months to do so. But based on her income and expenses, she actually only has $300 per month to save. This could be problematic for two reasons:

1. If she actually saved the $500 per month, either one (or more) of her bills would go unpaid; or she would need to pull the additional $200 from someplace else, meaning another need would go unmet, and she would most likely turn to increased credit card debt to fill the gap.

2. If the savings were just based on the remaining income of $300 per month, Vivica would have to save for 16+ months. Therefore, she would have to adjust her planning and timeline.

Hence, knowing and not guessing is essential for being able to plan for goals appropriately.

For budgeting to work and get you to true liberation, you must include all known expenses, not just some. For instance, you may include your transportation, housing, and grocery budget, but may not include your entertainment or fun expenses. That's not going to amount to an accurate budget.

To budget is to plan. To plan is to value your impact on the circumstances. In the budgeting process, you must know, not guess, your numbers. Knowledge is the beginning of liberation.

CHAPTER 1: RESOURCE DISCOVERY

"By failing to prepare, you are preparing to fail."
— Benjamin Franklin

Reviewing and knowing your current income and expenditures provides the foundation for the estimates you need to complete your budget.

THE RED CARPET GIRL

Kayla liked to purchase VIP access passes each time she attended a nightclub or concert. She enjoyed dressing up and being seen at high-end venues, but she also wanted to have a comfortable place to sit and relax while eating delicious food and watching the crowds. The passes cost $1,000 a pair.

I asked Kayla how often she purchased these passes. Over the course of a year, she explained, she would purchase the VIP package at least 15 times, resulting in a $15,000 entertainment expense.

As we reviewed her goals, Kayla mentioned that her desire was to pay off a $15,000 loan. I showed her that she already had the money in her budget to pay off the loan without working extra hours. By simply decreasing the number of VIP packages she purchased in a year, she could pay off the loan quickly. Kayla was shocked to learn this, as she had previously thought that paying off the debt was nearly impossible.

I explained that she didn't have to give up one important thing (the VIP passes) for another (paying off the debt). All she needed to do was shift her priorities for a time so she could responsibly reach a financial goal and still live the lifestyle she wanted. By knowing her income, expenses, and goals, and not guessing at them, Kayla was able to achieve an important goal.

The lesson here is to make sure the lifestyle priorities you set are in alignment with your financial priorities.

ESTIMATING

The estimation process consists of evaluating actual and potential sources of income and expenditures, then planning accordingly.

Here's how it's done. Review your bank statements and categorize the activity by using three categories:

1) Fixed expenses
2) Variable expenses
3) Income

FIXED EXPENSE

A fixed expense is something you pay for on a regular basis that is the same cost each time. A good example of this is your rent payment. For most people, the monthly rent is the same from month to month, although it could change from one year to the next, depending on whether the landlord decides to increase it.

Fixed Expense Table

Month	Rent Expense
January	$1,200
February	$1,200
March	$1,200
April	$1,200

VARIABLE EXPENSE

A variable expense is something you pay for on a regular basis, but the cost is often different depending on certain activity. An example of this is your heating bill. In the summer, the bill is typically lower than in the fall and winter months when you use the heat more often.

Variable Expense Table

Month	Heating Expense
August	$25
September	$32
October	$67
November	$98
December	$146

INCOME

You receive income in exchange for your work or as a result of your investments of time and effort. This generally refers to money received on a regular basis, but is not exclusive to this notion. Unemployment payments, taxable scholarship income, alimony, and social security benefits also fall under the income category, as do sale of products you produce and/or distribute, services you provide as an entrepreneur or as a side gig, or money earned from investments.

LIFESTYLE STORY

▸ OPTIMIZING FAMILY LIFE

James was making $40,000 per year, and his wife Jan made $35,000. Two college graduates with a household income of $75,000 provided a decent living in Southern California. They had two cars, an expensive apartment, and relative freedom in their spending habits. Then they got pregnant.

Suddenly, there were a few paths to choose: they could fit the baby into their lifestyle or they could change their lifestyle for their baby. Under this umbrella was a mix of options with different costs, some of them being: nursing vs. formula, homemaking vs. daycare/family, and working from home vs. working from the office.

Jan had always dreamed of being a stay-at-home mom, so she and James decided to change their lifestyle for their baby.

> They made it work with one car in support of a larger goal. James also focused more at work, planned more, thought about money, and revamped his resume in an effort to excel and make this lifestyle work. As a result of stewardship, budgeting, and promotions, they were able to afford a new car, move two miles from work, and still enjoy their lifestyle as parents.
>
> They learned what was important: Jan raising the baby and James providing was what worked for them. Ultimately, they achieved their goal.

With these definitions established, you are now ready to categorize and organize your bank statements. Technology has simplified this task via online banking. Statements can be downloaded to your program of choice, Microsoft Excel CSV files being the most common. By downloading these statements, you can look at all of your expenses and income sources in one place.

Start with one month of data. This process may initially be overwhelming, but it is worth the effort, and will quickly become fairly easy and routine. Starting with just one month will keep the data to a minimum.

The following example shows two tables: Financial Data illustrating debits and credits you may experience during a two-week period of time, including standard categories—income, fixed expenses, variable expenses, and liabilities; and a Pivot Table which indicates amounts allocated towards income, fixed expenses, variable expense, and liability for the same time period.

Example
Financial Data Table

Date	Amount	Category	Details
6/30/2014	($77.83)	Fixed	Insurance
6/29/2014	($120.65)	Liability	Student Loans
6/29/2014	($350.00)	Liability	Car Note
6/29/2014	($200.00)	Variable	Grocery Store
6/29/2014	($50.00)	Variable	Dinner Date
6/28/2014	($55.00)	Fixed	Cell Phone
6/28/2014	($1,200.00)	Liability	Mortgage
6/28/2014	($150.00)	Variable	Gas
6/22/2014	($3,500.00)	Income	Paycheck
6/21/2014	($45.00)	Fixed	Gym
6/20/2014	($45.00)	Variable	Utilities
6/19/2014	($65.00)	Fixed	Amusment Park Pass
6/18/2014	($75.00)	Fixed	Cable/Satellite
6/18/2014	($125.00)	Variable	Credit Card Payment

Pivot Table

Category	Amount
Fixed	($318)
Income	$3,500
Liability	($1,671)
Variable	($570)
Net Income	$942

ASSIGNMENT:

All assignment resources can be found at www.goaldiggersclub.com/membership-homepage/budgeting-resources/

1. Visit: www.goaldiggersclub.com/membership-homepage/budgeting-resources/ and click on budget book examples to download blank copies of the standard financial charts shown above. Fill in your own income and expenses to get a general snapshot of your financial picture.
   - How would you further categorize your expenses and liabilities?
   - Which expenses and liabilities can be adjusted easily?

2. Download the Needs vs. Wants Worksheet shown below. In the left column, list your wants, and use the right column to list your needs. Use the following definitions:
   - Want: Something that is desired, but not necessary to live.
   - Need: Something that is necessary to live a healthy, productive, enjoyable life.

3. Review each element in the list and ask yourself if you could survive without the items in the Wants column for 3 to 6 months. When answering the question, consider how the item plays a role in maintaining your livelihood. Also, decide how the item supports your sense of peace, health, and wellbeing. Make adjustments as necessary.

4. Go through each item in your Needs column and list the approximate cost for the item.

5. Review each item in your Wants column and assign the approximate cost.

6. Answer the following questions:
   - Are all of my needs fully funded? How can I reallocate spending from the Wants column to pay for more items in the Needs column?
   - Do I have any outstanding debt or liabilities? If yes, which items in the Needs column can be postponed, discounted, or adjusted so I can apply that money to pay down the liabilities?

Wants vs. Needs Table

Wants	Approx Cost	Needs	Approx Cost
A Porsche		Roof Over Our Head (aka pay the mortgage)	
An Electric Fireplace		Groceries	
A New Desk (even though the one I have now is perfectly acceptable)		Get An Oil Change	
Crown Molding		Cat Litter	
Mega Millions Lottery Ticket			

Using a new Needs vs. Wants Worksheet, rank the list of needs and wants in order based on the monthly cost of each. Does the final ranking reflect the priority that each item has in your life?

Now that you have discovered these resources, you can improve your personal financial position through planning and action. For example, canceling an unused $15 per month service and investing that money or using it to pay down debt could be an option for achieving your lifestyle goal. Although $180 annually doesn't seem like much, it can be used for a vehicle maintenance expense, addition to an investment fund, holiday or birthday gifts, or even to pay down a small debt.

Knowledge of your personal financial position is a valuable resource, whether your goal is to pay your credit card balance or to take a weekend trip. This is the beginning of your budget in action, the beginning of your journey to financial liberation. The same process can be done with your investment and retirement accounts. The goal is to understand your complete current financial position.

FINAL THOUGHT

The journey to financial liberation begins with understanding your current financial position. Having practical insight into your personal financial situation is imperative for managing your money and living the life you want. When you don't know where you stand financially, you limit your ability to be your best self. By taking the time to understand and recognize things like current and speculative income, fixed and variable expenses, as well as long- and short-term liabilities, you are liberating yourself and making it possible to pursue your dreams.

CHAPTER 2: GATHERING EXPERIENCE

"Experience is the teacher of all things."
– Julius Caesar

You learn by doing. Practical experience is invaluable. Just being shown or told what to do isn't the same as actually doing it yourself. You will likely make mistakes with many experiences in life, but over time your skills will improve and they will become second nature. The same goes for budgeting.

Budgeting isn't a one-time event. As you continue to refine your budgeting process you will begin to make adjustments for unique changes in your personal situation. Your first budget won't be flawless and all encompassing, which is okay. A personal budget should be adjusted and continuously tailored to your life, especially as your life changes and your understanding of budgeting increases.

There are four basic types of budgets:
1. Time Period Forecast—a budget indicating expected income and expenses for a specific time period (typically a month or a quarter);
2. 80/20 Budget—a budget where you save 20 percent and live off 80 percent of your income;
3. Broad Percentage Method—a budget showing your expense categories as percentages of total expenses. (Generally 5 to 7 categories are sufficient).
4. Straight-Line Budget—one of the simplest to understand and use. (This type of budget will be explored further in this chapter).

STRAIGHT-LINE BUDGET

A straight-line budget allocates your annual income and expenses evenly across the year for simplicity, rather than showing fluctuations and miscellaneous details that occur month to month in a normal year.

For example, if you are paid bi-weekly, there are 26 pay periods in a year. Some months will have three paychecks while others will have two. Again, the Straight-Line Budget does not account for fluctuations in income or expenses. For example, winter months require more gas usage to heat your home, resulting in higher bills. On the income side, if you have a varying work schedule, as do many teachers or other seasonal employees, you may have to account for fluctuations in income. These changes are not typically noted in this type of budget.

 **Budgeting is a part of smart planning, and planning will help you reach your goals and achieve your dreams.**

Revolving Expenses

	Jan	Feb	Mar	Apr	May	Jun	Jul	Aug	Sept	Oct	Nov	Dec	Total
Student Loans	$222	$222	$222	$222	$222	$222	$222	$222	$222	$222	$222	$222	$2,664
Credit Card	$78	$78	$78	$78	$78	$78	$78	$78	$78	$78	$78	$78	$936
Cable/ Satellite	$120	$120	$120	$120	$120	$120	$120	$120	$120	$120	$120	$120	$1,440
Netflix/ Hulu	$20	$20	$20	$20	$20	$20	$20	$20	$20	$20	$20	$20	$240
Rent/ Mortgage	$900	$900	$900	$900	$900	$900	$900	$900	$900	$900	$900	$900	$10,800
Utilities	$50	$50	$50	$50	$50	$50	$50	$50	$50	$50	$50	$50	$600
Car Insurance	$80	$80	$80	$80	$80	$80	$80	$80	$80	$80	$80	$80	$960
Car Note	$300	$300	$300	$300	$300	$300	$300	$300	$300	$300	$300	$300	$3,600
Gym	$40	$40	$40	$40	$40	$40	$40	$40	$40	$40	$40	$40	$480
Cell Phone	$50	$50	$50	$50	$50	$50	$50	$50	$50	$50	$50	$50	$600
Total	$1,860	$1,860	$1,860	$1,860	$1,860	$1,860	$1,860	$1,860	$1,860	$1,860	$1,860	$1,860	$22,320

chapter 2: gathering experience

Variable Expenses

	Jan	Feb	Mar	Apr	May	Jun	Jul	Aug	Sept	Oct	Nov	Dec	Total
Fuel/Toll	$200	$200	$200	$200	$200	$200	$200	$200	$200	$200	$200	$200	$2,400
Groceries	$250	$250	$250	$250	$250	$250	$250	$250	$250	$250	$250	$250	$3,000
Restaurants	$100	$100	$100	$100	$100	$100	$100	$100	$100	$100	$100	$100	$1,200
*Miscella-neous	$200	$200	$200	$200	$200	$200	$200	$200	$200	$200	$200	$200	$2,400
Total	$750	$750	$750	$750	$750	$750	$750	$750	$750	$750	$750	$750	$9,000
$50K - Flat, After Tax	$3,333	$3,333	$3,333	$3,333	$3,333	$3,333	$3,333	$3,333	$3,333	$3,333	$3,333	$3,333	$3,333
Profit/Loss YTD	$723	$1,447	$2,170	$2,893	$3,617	$4,340	$5,063	$5,787	$6,510	$7,233	$7,957	$8,680	$8,680
Raise - 3% Mar	$3,433	$3,433	$3,433	$3,433	$3,433	$3,433	$3,433	$3,433	$3,433	$3,433	$3,433	$3,433	$41,000
Profit/Loss YTD	$723	$1,447	$2,270	$3,093	$3,917	$4,740	$5,563	$6,387	$7,210	$8,033	$8,857	$9,680	$9,680
Raise - 3% Mar, 4% Nov	$3,333	$3,333	$3,433	$3,433	$3,433	$3,433	$3,433	$3,433	$3,433	$3,433	$3,571	$3,571	$41,275
Profit/Loss YTD	$723	$1,447	$2,270	$3,093	$3,917	$4,740	$5,563	$6,387	$7,210	$8,033	$8,994	$9,955	$9,955

*Car registration and maintenance, personal shopping, birthdays and holidays, toiletries, etc.

chapter 2: gathering experience

CASE STUDY 1: AM I READY TO BUY A HOME?

Budget Details and Assumptions
Goal: Home purchase in December

Evaluate your fixed expenses, variable expenses, and income within your budget to determine if you can purchase a home at the end of the year. To determine if you can purchase a home, you will evaluate three income options:

1. Salary remains flat all year with no merit increase;
2. 3 percent merit salary increase on March 1st;
3. 3 percent merit salary increase on March 1st and 4 percent promotion salary increase on November 1st.

You will find your list of inputs below.
Type of Budget: Straight-Line
Period: One calendar year

Fixed Expense: Continue prior year spending habits with changes dependent upon three budget scenarios: Fixed, based on prior year spending habits as shown in the Straight-Line Budget example.

Variable Expense: Fixed, based on prior year spending habits as shown in the Straight-Line Budget example.

Income: Remain fully employed for the duration of the year with three income budget scenarios:

1. Salary remains flat;
2. 3 percent merit salary increase on March 1st;
3. 3 percent merit salary increase on March 1st and 4 percent promotion salary increase on November 1st.

QUESTIONS:

- Can you purchase the home under income scenario 1—no salary increase? If so, what changes do you need to make in your budget to purchase the home?
- Can you purchase the home under income scenario 2—3% merit increase? If so, what changes do you need to make in your budget to purchase the home?
- Can you purchase the home under income scenario 3—3% merit increase and promotion? If so, what changes do you need to make in your budget to purchase the home?

Visit: www.goaldiggersclub.com/membership-homepage/budgeting-resources/ to download a blank Straight-Line Budget template you can fill in using your own numbers.

The estimation for this one-year budget is that all other income and fixed and variable expenses will remain unchanged unless two conditions are met:

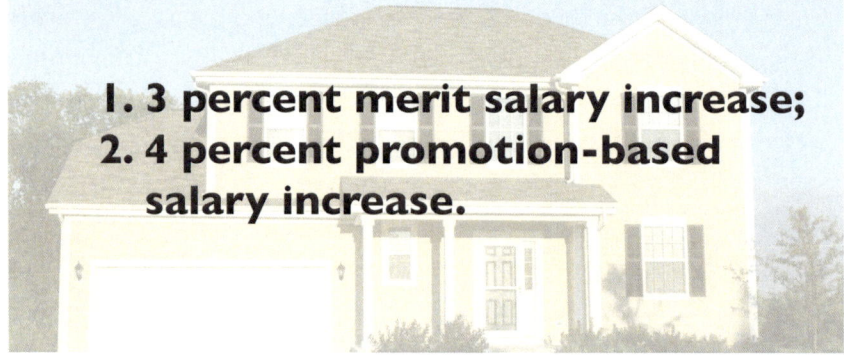

1. 3 percent merit salary increase;
2. 4 percent promotion-based salary increase.

Only if these two conditions are met would you actually purchase the home. By using principles of wise planning and patience, the home purchase decision is triggered by factual income increases

28 chapter 2: gathering experience

and overall affordability, not by external indicators such as lower housing prices, low mortgage interest rates, a friend's home purchase ("keeping up with the Joneses"), or a new family member (a new baby, or a parent or sibling moving in). This will allow you to remain as objective as possible when making your final decision.

Again, this is a simplistic example to give an introduction to the subject matter. If you are between jobs, planning for school, self-employed, working in real estate, or having income fluctuations, your process will be less simple.

This Straight-Line Budget can be modified for different time periods and projections; however, start with this simple example and build your one-year budget from there, using information gathered from your bank statement. Use your month of categorized data to produce estimates for the rest of the year. The point is to know your financial standing and annual estimates so you can begin planning for larger accomplishments.

Some purchases, such as a car or a home, require upfront payments. In this example, if you had $11,000 in savings at the beginning of the year, by the end of the year you would have enough for a down payment on your new house if you indeed got the promotion and salary increase. If you did not have enough saved, you would have to wait a while longer and purchase the home when your budget illustrates that the purchase is both feasible and realistic.

Compare the budget in the example to the budget you created for yourself. You now have a Straight-Line budget to start managing your money. Use it. This is the experience you need to become comfortable with the budgeting process: how to create a budget, adjust it, and make decisions based on what it indicates. The only way you'll know for sure whether you can improve your financial situation is by addressing it head on.

AVOID DEFERRED HAPPINESS

Most Americans live with a deferred happiness goal, meaning that they put off experiences that will make them happy until circumstances allow for them. Most times, this never happens. Is this the standard by which you want to live? If not, you can plan to experience whatever you want in life. Remember, budgeting is a part of smart planning, and planning will help you reach your goals and achieve your dreams.

Budgeting allows you to eliminate the stress of purchasing items and investing in fulfilling experiences. Budgeting helps make those experiences more satisfying and less burdensome. For this reason, budgeting is important when determining what you need to live a full and balanced life. Budgeting allows you to wisely decide what to purchase based on your pre-determined criteria and goals. Budgeting frees you from spending your life working hard with the hope of relaxing later.

LIFESTYLE STORY

▸ INTERNATIONAL TEACHING EXPERIENCE

April was always a focused and determined teacher and an avid traveler. By studying abroad with the Semester at Sea program in college, she decided to volunteer her time to underserved communities throughout the world. In the States, she used her talents in a school system for underprivileged students. She was determined to expose those kids who had never been out of their community to new experiences.

She looked at her salary and realized this was not a goal she could accomplish on her own. So she created a budget and a plan that outlined costs, education, funding, and program benefits.

She pitched the idea to several institutions and programs throughout New York and internationally, and obtained sponsor funding. As a result, during her first year as a teacher, she was able to take a small group of students to South America. After that, she used her experience and results to take students all over the world. Not only did she get the satisfaction of educating and exposing students to entirely different perspectives, she was able to satisfy her love of travel and fulfill her own self-worth without needing additional resources in her personal budget.

FINAL THOUGHT

Review your budget at different times and from various perspectives to ensure it is of most value to you. Start with the simple Straight-Line budget to become comfortable with structuring your finances, and expand it over time.

CHAPTER 3: FROM DATA TO KNOWLEDGE

"The goal is to transform data into information, and information into insight."
— Carly Fiorina

Your financial transactions are data. How you categorize this data is information. How your finances fit into your life is knowledge. If you've never thought of financial information as knowledge, consider this explanation:

Think about your own bank account. Whether you actively manage it or not, you know you can check every day to see where your money is going. You can look at deposits, withdrawals, payments, and purchases you've made. You can also check on any fees or other miscellaneous charges in your account. At the least, you can check at any given moment to see how much money you have.

When you check your account, you see a list of figures. Those figures represent raw data as it relates to your finances. But viewing a list of numbers doesn't really mean much without additional context. Your bank statement includes categories and descriptions to provide that context.

There are typically a minimum of four different ways those figures are categorized on your bank statement: withdrawal/debit, deposit/credit, date, description/name of company. By considering those figures in the context of these categories, you are equipped to have a much deeper understanding of them. Those categories turn the data (figures) into information. By reviewing them as relating to your personal situation, you will gain the knowledge necessary to plan and properly manage your lifestyle.

Don't view your banking information as a group of numbers and unnecessary figures. Rather, view it as data that becomes information when organized and categorized. The numbers aren't there to overwhelm you. They're there to educate you.

To become liberated, you need a plan. To construct a plan, you need knowledge of your personal financial situation, as was illustrated in Case Study 1. If you don't have a predisposition toward numbers, looking at your own financial information can be overwhelming. Categorizing helps clarify your financial picture so you can better understand the numbers.

You probably have a general sense of the money you have, or don't have, on a monthly basis. However, you should endeavor to be more specific in your understanding of your financial position. Here are a few questions you should be able to answer:

- What is my total monthly income?
- What is my total of monthly expenditures?
- How much of my monthly expenditures are funded with debt (credit cards, loans, or other borrowed money)?
- What is my ideal amount of monthly expenditures funded with debt?
- How much of my income is spent on food and entertainment per month?
- What is my ideal amount spent on food and entertainment per month?
- What are my tax withholdings? For W2 employees, you can probably find these on the payment stub of your paycheck. They include social security, Medicare, federal income taxes, and potentially state income taxes that employers deduct [withhold] from

each paycheck and are the difference between gross income and net income.
- What is the difference between my gross income and my net income?

Answering the above questions will help you become knowledgeable about your financial situation so you can plan wisely. Wisdom is the combination of knowledge, experience, and discernment. Seek ways to make adjustments to help you reach your goals.

Soon you will begin to ask yourself the following questions to help you spend less and save more to reach your goals more quickly and with little or no stress:

- What steps can I take to lower my credit card interest rate, insurance rate, gym rate, or cell phone rate?
- Am I willing to cook more, eat less, exercise outside the gym, or use cash instead of credit?
- What can I do now to ensure I have enough money to live comfortably when I retire?
- How much of my income am I willing to use to reduce debt?

Upon answering these types of questions, you will find yourself in a better position to answer questions such as:

- How often would I like to take a vacation each year?
- What adjustments to my lifestyle do I need to make to buy a new car in the next year?
- How disciplined am I willing to be with my spending and saving so I can quit my job and go back to school?

chapter 3: from data to knowledge

You may wonder why you need to ask yourself these questions. You may also wonder why you need to pay bills at a certain time every month and why you need money at all. The truth of the matter is that we live in a time when people use currency to navigate through life.

In order to maximize the use of currency, you need to know exactly what your current financial situation is and what you want it to be in the future. If you would like to replace your car in one year, but the reality of your financial situation illustrates that this goal will take two years, you should know this so you can make other plans or adjustments to your budget based on this goal.

You have control of your entire life. You have the choice to change or to keep things as they are. When you consider making a change, you first need to know what is important to you. Based on your priorities, your personal financial decisions become easy to comprehend and carry through.

Knowing your priorities also helps you discover if you're making financial decisions in accordance with your stated goals. For instance, you may have decided that your intellectual pursuits are vital to your overall balance and life happiness. Ideally, you would like to go back to school full-time; however, you haven't figured out how to fund your lifestyle without working while attending school.

In reviewing your priorities, you realize that attending school is more important than not attending school. As such, you decide to start your graduate degree program part-time and transition to full-time after the second year. This process enables you to make the decisions you need to move forward instead of waiting or deferring your dream.

These questions are easy to put off when you don't have a clear idea of your financial situation. Answering the first set of questions gives you the freedom to consider the second set of questions. And knowing the answers to all of them illustrates how data becomes information, and information becomes knowledge.

CASE STUDY 2: THANKS/NO THANKS, MOM AND DAD

Many parents offer to pay for their children's college expenses. That may sound nice at first, but unfortunately, many parents are ill-prepared to fully fund a four-year college education. This astronomical financial commitment includes tuition, books, housing, food, transportation, and more.

Recent figures by The College Board®[1] project the four-year tuition fees at a private college to be $134,600 and at a public university (in-state student) to be $39,400. At an increased rate of 3.8 percent for private colleges and 2.9 percent for public universities over the previous year, that amount could break the budget of practically any family.

Aaron decided to study accounting at a public university. He was ecstatic when his parents agreed to pay the $5,000 per year tuition. Upon graduation, he decided to extend his education and attend graduate school at a private university in another state. This amounted to ten times the cost, or $50,000 per year. This time, Aaron's parents were unable to commit to footing the bill, leaving Aaron with a few options:

1. Go into debt to pay for grad school;
2. Attend a school with lower tuition fees;
3. Find other funding options to pay for his college education.

1- Family Guide to College Savings, "The real cost of higher education," Savingforcollege.com (http://www.savingforcollege.com/tutorial101/the_real_cost_of_higher_education.php: accessed 3 Feb 2015).

Obviously, if Aaron and his parents had known (and not guessed) the cost of college and their ability to pay the required fees, they would have been in a better position to see Aaron achieve his goal of earning an advanced degree. Instead, they had to consider other options at a time that was essentially inconvenient for Aaron.

The lesson here is to plan ahead for large expenses. Taking the time early on to anticipate costs, payment plans, and additional funding options could save you time and headache in the long term.

LIFESTYLE STORY

▶ SEEING THE WORLD WHILE PAYING OFF STUDENT DEBT

Dionne was always a free spirit guided by love and adventure. She often found herself living in exotic and beautiful destinations. Dionne was never attached to possessions or resistant to change. However, she looked at her student loan debt balance and realized that in order to pay off the loans for her MBA, she needed to make some changes.

She researched several options, including getting a corporate job and changing her entire lifestyle so she could get out of debt completely. However, she decided that the quickest way was an option she had not previously considered. She quit her job as a Spanish teacher, went to a Navy recruitment facility, and joined the military. At the end of her four-year commitment she was debt free, and had experienced living in other countries while gaining additional skills to propel her into a higher-paying field of work.

ASSIGNMENT:

1. Download the Wealthy Yogi Lifestyle Assessment from www.goaldiggersclub.com/membership-homepage/budgeting-resources/

2. For each element in the Assessment, rate your current assessment of yourself by selecting a value between 1 and 10. For instance, for the "helping others" category, if you donate your time in a way that completely satisfies your need to give, you would rate yourself as a 10 in that category. In contrast, if you really love to read every day and you haven't read a book in an entire year, you may rate your intellectual pursuit area as the value of 2 out of 10.

chapter 3: from data to knowledge

3. Next, list your top three priorities in each category. If you have fewer than three, you're on the right track.

4. Review your budget and priorities, and decide if you are allocating too much, too little, or the right amount to each category in your wheel.

5. From the areas you select as over allocation, determine possible ways to reallocate any excess to the categories in which you have added too little.

Everyone's situation is different. This is just one method to help you arrive at your own custom solution so you feel empowered to begin making changes. You might need help from a financial planner, tax consultant, or retirement counselor to carry out your plan. However, having knowledge of your situation is an important starting point. With this, you can begin planning and can get one step closer to liberation.

FINAL THOUGHT

Review your budget at different times and from various perspectives to ensure it is of most value to you. Start with the simple straight-line budget to become comfortable with structuring your finances, and expand it over time.

PART TWO: TO PLAN, NOT HOPE

*"Desire is the starting point of all achievement,
not a hope, not a wish, but a keen pulsating
desire which transcends everything."*
— Napoleon Hill

The mechanics of budgeting follow the well-known practice of shifting thoughts to actions and values. Practices such as setting yearly goals, creating vision boards, and surrounding yourself with like-minded people lend themselves to reaching greater success. Yet many people ditch these tried and true principles in favor of just hoping everything will work out. Although positivity goes a long way, coupling positivity with right planning gives you a purposeful push in the right direction.

Before creating your first simple budget, think about your perception of the budgeting process. Your relationship with money can be a tenuous one, largely marked by fear and uncertainty, but it doesn't have to be. When you change your perception of budgeting as a restrictive process and redefine words related to money and budgeting you might find yourself more willing to embrace the process.

The shift begins with your perception about budgeting.

CHAPTER 4: SHIFTING YOUR PERCEPTION

"Your beliefs become your thoughts, your thoughts become your words, your words become your actions, your actions become your habits, your habits become your values, your values become your destiny."
– Mahatma Gandhi

There is freedom in being able to clearly and honestly evaluate yourself, your environment, and your situation. Budgeting helps you do this with your finances. Rather than believing that the only correct way to manage your finances is the way you've always done it—the way your parents managed their money, or the way you're currently doing it—begin to open your mind to accept other ways to perceive your money management.

If you were already doing everything correctly why would you need to do anything differently—ever? You wouldn't. No performance reviews at your job; no chastisement from the dentist for not brushing properly; no motivation from your personal trainer to get back into the gym. But you know this isn't the case. So being open to the reality that there is always room for improvement is a necessary step toward seeing the change you want. But you have to decide to make a change.

FEAR-BASED DECISION MAKING

Unfortunately, many people make decisions based on fear and past bad experiences—their own or someone else's. For instance, you might select a job you don't like over a job you do like simply because you believe it has more financial security. Or you might be reluctant to take much-needed vacation time because you are afraid your boss or coworkers will devalue your commitment to your work. Or you might buy designer clothing and accessories because you fear losing your social standing without these items.

As dictated by practically every major religion and living philosophy, no decisions should be made based on fear of a particular outcome; unless, of course, you're faced with imminent danger. You must remember this principle when managing your money. Do not allow fear to impact your earning potential, spending, saving, investing, and overall quality of life.

> **Do not allow fear to impact your overall quality of life.**

In order to prevent fear-based decision making, make decisions based on your passion and priorities, not on the expected outcome. After all, you cannot control the outcome of your financial decisions. You can only control your intention. So make an intention to have the best life you can by making smarter financial decisions.

MANAGING MONEY REQUIRES RESOURCEFULNESS

The greatest commodity in our current economy is resourcefulness. By definition, a commodity is something that is marketable and able to satisfy a need or want. You use your income resources to satisfy the elements listed in your Needs vs. Wants exercise.

In addition to external resourcefulness, there is also internal resourcefulness. With internal resources you may be able to look inward to decide if you really need everything on your Needs vs. Wants sheet. Decreasing the need for outside goods and services and increasing your internal resourcefulness are great strategies to satisfying your needs and wants.

In business, the "do more with less" philosophy is commonplace. Unfortunately, in personal finance, many people are misguided about how to make resourceful decisions. In contrast to the business sector, individuals effectively operate with a "do less with less" mentality.

For example, with the goal of saving time (yet at the expense of higher cost), you might frequent fast food and dine-in restaurants instead of grocery stores. By doing this you probably end up spending more money, having less quality time with your loved ones, and sacrificing your health. In fact, you might not realize that convenience comes with a premium price.

Relatively small changes in your resourcefulness can return large improvements to your results. For instance, cooking two meals a week while also eating the leftovers for lunch can save money. Learning how to cook, to manage personal/familial grooming, to change engine oil, or to properly plan can go a long way toward reaching your financial goals.

But for resourcefulness to have the most benefit, you have to back it up with consistent action.

ACTIVE DILIGENCE

Money is one area that can cause stress in your life. This stress is often due to lack of control. If you find yourself in a situation where you are barely making ends meet or are faced with a financial burden you don't have the money to cover, you can feel helpless.

Living paycheck to paycheck is stressful. Feeling as if you're always playing catch-up is stressful and limits your ability to enjoy all that life has to offer.

Budgeting when you are scrambling to stay afloat can be tough. But budgeting can be most beneficial during difficult financial circumstances. Budgeting gives you the ability to better manage stress caused by financial challenges. Knowing what you can and cannot afford at any given time can help reduce your stress. Knowing for certain you can't maintain your current lifestyle is much better than erroneously assuming you can.

Crafting and executing a budget isn't only for people with extra income or a large bank account. In fact, if you have a limited supply of money you could actually gain more freedom from having a budget than from not having one. Budgeting gives you control and practical knowledge about where you stand financially.

You'd be surprised at how much money you do have when you take the time to categorize and organize it. Hoping and wishing things will get better when you find a new job, win the lottery, or get that raise you've been working toward isn't a solid plan. Budgeting gives you a plan. By taking the time to outline your expenses and compare them to your income, you can take a realistic look at your financial situation and plan accordingly. This is active diligence.

Just like you would perform due diligence before investing in property or purchasing stock shares, be actively diligent about your budgeting. Do your homework and finish what you start.

MY STORY

Throughout my life and my career, I've had to shift my perception about budgeting, taking into account each of the areas mentioned in this chapter: fear-based decision making, resourcefulness, and active diligence.

When I worked as an engineer in corporate America, I had a goal of obtaining the title of Director so I could reach what I thought was the ultimate level of financial security and not have to worry about money. I worked hard at the consulting company where I was employed. I collaborated with key people, impressed the right decision makers, and received glowing feedback from my clients. As a result, I was offered a position as Director. My first two questions after receiving the offer were:

1. What is the salary increase?
2. How will my job requirements change?

I was told the job change would be in title only. I was also told I would be assessed based on how much I could grow my business area in terms of billables and contract significance. I was extremely disappointed. I would have to leave my favorite part of the work, completing risk analyses, to become a full-time business development director. Moreover, I would not gain any additional financial stability. Lastly, I wouldn't even get a raise by taking such a risk for leaving my comfort zone as an engineer. At that point in my career, my priorities weren't met, so I turned down the promotion.

Some might view my decision as a bold move, but for me it wasn't. Why? Because I had a budget that was designed to help me reach my goals and to live my ideal lifestyle by guiding my daily expense activities based on my current income. I was not motivated by fear. I employed financial resourcefulness. I practiced active diligence when it came to my budgeting. Therefore, I was able to not only turn down the promotion, but also eventually to leave that company and corporate America.

My need for job-based security has changed since then, and I'm now a full-time entrepreneur. I was able to accomplish this because

I made decisions based on who I was at the time, not based on the past me, or my ideal self, or even my hopes for the future. I knew my priorities, and I created and executed a plan to move forward accordingly. I did so with my secret weapon: wise thoughtfulness.

WISE THOUGHTFULNESS

Hoping and wishing your financial situation will improve is not a plan. Playing the lottery or gambling is not a plan. Many people go through life hoping and wishing for a windfall where they will end up wealthy and all their money woes will go out the window. That is not a plan either.

Numbers are hard proof of your decision-making ability. You can't deal with them by fervently wishing and hoping things will ultimately get better. You must approach budgeting and financial planning with wise thoughtfulness.

Wisdom is using the knowledge and resources you have to take action. Thoughtfulness is considering all possible options before making a decision. Combining these two concepts is critical to making the budgeting process work for you, no matter what your financial situation.

Thinking that your situation cannot change is a perception, and ultimately, your reality. But is it correct? Is there action you can take, help you can seek, patience you can exhibit, things or people you can avoid, or someone you can meet who could help you improve your current circumstances? The answer is always, yes! But none of the aforementioned things can happen if you don't believe they can.

Don't get caught in the mindset that your life is hopeless, even if you have been taught to think in such a way. You can change your career. You can pay off your debt. You can retire without worries. You can transform your whole life if you believe your dreams are worth it.

LIFESTYLE STORY

▸ STARTING A BUSINESS

Lora did everything she was supposed to do. She completed her bachelor and master degrees, and was awarded a coveted job at a prestigious corporation. She worked both strategically and diligently, and became a Director in her company by the age of 27. But with all her success, the job did not fulfill her search for happiness. She decided to consider entrepreneurial opportunities and strike out on her own.

An avid saver, Lora generally saved 15 to 20 percent of her income. She read books about entrepreneurship and accepted the reality that she would need to save about 1 to 2 years of living expenses to get her through the first two years as a business owner. As a result, she decided to contribute the maximum to her 401(k) account. In addition, she drastically reduced her monthly expenses so she could increase her business fund. That way she would not have to worry about personal living expenses while in the start-up phase of her business.

After doing this for a year, she decided she was ready to take a leap of faith and start her own business. She was both hopeful and nervous, but she figured the worst-case scenario would be going back to corporate America with a brand new set of skills to apply to her working environment.

> Like everyone, she only had one life to lead. Lora decided she wanted a life where she believed in herself enough to try to reach her goals and not to let fear dictate her choices. Lora is still figuring out business management efficiencies, but she loves the freedom she has in directing her own life every day.

FINAL THOUGHT

Sure, everyone pays their bills, takes a vacation with a credit card, and buys a car, or maybe a house. But few people sit down and talk about (or with) their money. With the help of your budget, you will create a conversation with your finances. This might sound odd, and it is not to suggest that you actually speak to your dollar bills or your credit cards. But consider that your finances are your employees; they work for you, so you have the power to direct their effort and focus so they accomplish the goals and dreams you have planned for yourself.

CHAPTER 5: HANDS-ON BUDGET PLANNING

*"If you don't know where you are going,
you'll end up someplace else."*
— Yogi Berra

Creating a useful, realistic budget is a process that requires observation, self-analysis, and action. Remember that your budget will change as your circumstances change. Being actively engaged with your budget is critical to achieving liberation. Hands-on planning is essential in the budgeting process.

Now it's time to roll up your sleeves and create your own budget.

Creating your budget will put you in the right mindset and provide experience for achieving your personal objectives. This 5-step budget creation process includes the following steps:

1. Track and Observe;
2. Perform a Budgeting Makeover;
3. Start Your Emergency Fund;
4. Pay Down Your Debt;
5. Complete Your Emergency Fund.

Begin by completing the Comprehensive Personal Monthly Budget. Download a blank Personal Monthly Budget worksheet at www.goaldiggersclub.com/membership-homepage/budgeting-resources/

Personal Monthly Budget

Projected Monthly Income	
Income 1 - Pay 1st	$
Income 2 - Pay 15th	$
Total monthly income	$
Actual Monthly Income	
Income 1 - Pay 1st	$
Income 2 - Pay 15th	$
Income 3 - Extra Income	$
Total monthly income	$

Housing	Projected Cost	Actual Cost	Difference
Mortgage or rent	$	$	$
Mobile Phone	$	$	$
Electricity	$	$	$
Gas	$	$	$
Water and sewer	$	$	$
Cable	$	$	$
Waste removal	$	$	$
Internet	$	$	$
Furnishings	$	$	$
Supplies	$	$	$
HOA Dues	$	$	$
Subtotals	$	$	$

Transportation	Projected Cost	Actual Cost	Difference
Vehicle payment	$	$	$
Insurance	$	$	$
Parking	$	$	$
Public Transportation	$	$	$
Licensing	$	$	$
Fuel	$	$	$
Maintenance Fund	$	$	$
Taxes & Registration	$	$	$
Subtotals	$	$	$

Personal Monthly Budget

Insurance	Projected Cost	Actual Cost	Difference
Homeowners Insurance	$	$	$
Health Insurance	$	$	$
Disability Insurance	$	$	$
Dental Insurance	$	$	$
Life Insurance	$	$	$
Other	$	$	$
Subtotals	$	$	$

Food	Projected Cost	Actual Cost	Difference
Groceries	$	$	$
Dining out	$	$	$
Other/Bars	$	$	$
Coffee	$	$	$
Subtotals	$	$	$

Personal Care	Projected Cost	Actual Cost	Difference
Medical	$	$	$
Hair + Salon	$	$	$
Clothing	$	$	$
Dry cleaning	$	$	$
Shopping	$	$	$
Subscriptions	$	$	$
Health club	$	$	$
Organization dues or fees	$	$	$
Other	$	$	$
Subtotals	$	$	$

chapter 5: hands-on budget planning

Personal Monthly Budget

Pets	Projected Cost	Actual Cost	Difference
Food	$	$	$
Medical	$	$	$
Grooming	$	$	$
Toys	$	$	$
Other	$	$	$
Subtotals	$	$	$

Entertainment	Projected Cost	Actual Cost	Difference
Video/DVD	$	$	$
CDs	$	$	$
Movies	$	$	$
Concerts	$	$	$
Sporting events	$	$	$
Other	$	$	$
Cash & ATM	$	$	$
Travel/Vacation	$	$	$
Other	$	$	$
Subtotals	$	$	$

Loans	Projected Cost	Actual Cost	Difference
Credit Card 1	$	$	$
Credit Card 2	$	$	$
Credit Card 3	$	$	$
Credit Card 4	$	$	$
Student Loan	$	$	$
Personal Loan	$	$	$
Subtotals	$	$	$

Education & Personal Development	Projected Cost	Actual Cost	Difference
Tuition + Fees	$	$	$
Education Supplies	$	$	$
Conferences	$	$	$
Subtotals	$	$	$

Personal Monthly Budget

Taxes	Projected Cost	Actual Cost	Difference
State	$	$	$
Local	$	$	$
Property	$	$	$
Subtotals	$	$	$

Savings or Investments	Projected Cost	Actual Cost	Difference
Retirement account Roth IRA	$	$	$
Investment account	$	$	$
Savings	$	$	$
Financial Planning	$	$	$
Subtotals	$	$	$

Gifts And Donations	Projected Cost	Actual Cost	Difference
Charity 1	$	$	$
Charity 2	$	$	$
Charity 3	$	$	$
Family & Friends Gifts	$	$	$
Subtotals	$	$	$

Legal	Projected Cost	Actual Cost	Difference
Attorney	$	$	$
Other	$	$	$
Subtotals	$	$	$

TOTAL PROJECTED COST	$
TOTAL ACTUAL COST	$
TOTAL DIFFERENCE	$

chapter 5: hands-on budget planning

Begin by completing the Comprehensive Personal Monthly Budget. Download a blank Personal Monthly Budget worksheet at www.goaldiggersclub.com/membership-homepage/budgeting-resources/

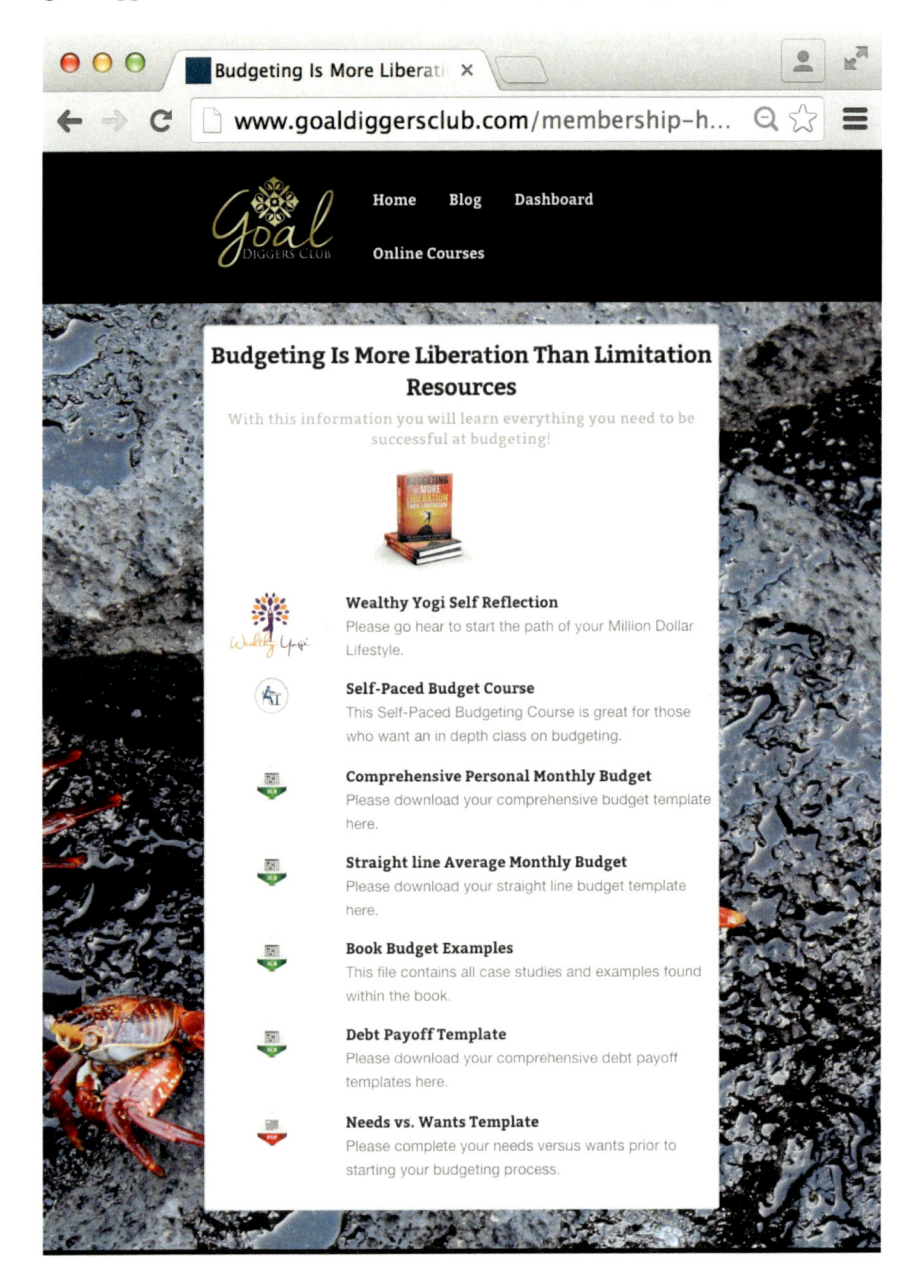

Budgeting Is More Liberation Than Limitation Resources

With this information you will learn everything you need to be successful at budgeting!

Wealthy Yogi Self Reflection
Please go hear to start the path of your Million Dollar Lifestyle.

Self-Paced Budget Course
This Self-Paced Budgeting Course is great for those who want an in depth class on budgeting.

Comprehensive Personal Monthly Budget
Please download your comprehensive budget template here.

Straight line Average Monthly Budget
Please download your straight line budget template here.

Book Budget Examples
This file contains all case studies and examples found within the book.

Debt Payoff Template
Please download your comprehensive debt payoff templates here.

Needs vs. Wants Template
Please complete your needs versus wants prior to starting your budgeting process.

STEP 1: TRACK AND OBSERVE

The first step is to observe and track your spending habits for 1 to 3 months. This will allow you to experience monitoring your financial life. By tracking your expenditures over a longer period, you can highlight some of your periodic and/or seasonal purchases. In addition, you can discover if your purchases match your values.

> **Your purchases must match your values.**

Unfortunately, many people spend money on items that are not important to them. It is critical that your spending matches your happiness, your goals, and your values. For instance, writers may spend money on book releases and literary conferences, whereas audiophiles may have a larger electronics budget. Your budget should be customized to your individual situation. The most important thing is that you eliminate wasteful spending.

Begin by eliminating the things that are on the bottom of your list. As you record your expenses during this 3-month period, make sure you compare expenses to your wants versus needs data to ensure that you're spending in alignment with your priorities.

STEP 2: PERFORM A BUDGETING MAKEOVER

Once you create an initial budget, you may need to complete a budget makeover. The budget makeover is necessary if you cannot reach your intended goals with your actual budget. For instance, if your expenses exceed your income you need to either increase your income or decrease your expenses to correct the imbalance.

Also, if you have specific financial goals that are not included in your current budget you will have to integrate them into your budget. For instance, if you want to attend Carnival in Brazil next year you will have to add this savings category to your budget to help guarantee you reach your financial objectives.

Some immediate ways to adjust your budget are:
- Negotiate with creditors;
- Negotiate utilities;
- Look into debt consolidation;
- Reduce interest rates;
- Save to buy.

STEP 3: START YOUR EMERGENCY FUND

An Emergency Fund is for unexpected expenses. This account will help prevent you from falling off your plan when minor financial emergencies arise, such as a flood in the basement, a car accident, or an unexpected health issue.

Once you have positive net income, the next step is to fund one month of emergency savings. This amount is equivalent to your monthly expenditures. To determine how long it will take to accumulate this amount, divide your total monthly expenditures by your total net income.

For example, if you need $1,000 for your monthly expenses and you have $100 net income per month, it will take 10 months to build your Emergency Fund.

$$\$1{,}000 \div \$100 = 10 \text{ months}$$

Your budget is designed for your specific situation. At minimum, your Emergency Fund should cover the most fundamental expenses, such as food and shelter.

STEP 4: PAY DOWN YOUR DEBT

Debt is a major part of the financial life of most every American. According to a July 2014 report by the Urban Institute,[2] the average total household debt in America is $53,850. For most people, debt is in the form of credit cards, mortgages, student loans, medical bills, unpaid utility bills, and other consumer loans. In the same study, among those with a credit history, the average non-mortgage debt stood at nearly $16,000 per person.

Debt may be part of the American culture, but it should not be part of your budget. Debt reduction and elimination is the first step to financial freedom.

As part of your budget, you should plan to pay down or pay off your debts with the payment method that works for you and your creditors. You can try to reduce interest rates, consolidate debt for a zero or low interest rate offer, or negotiate the amount of debt owed to a particular creditor.

Once you pay off one debt, apply any positive net income to your remaining debt payments using your chosen strategy. Possible strategies include:

- Debt Snowball—Pay down debt in order from smallest to largest amount. Once each debt is paid off, all positive net income plus paid-off payments are applied to the debt with the next smallest balance.

2- The Urban Institute, "Debt in America," (http://www.urban.org/UploadedPDF/413190-Debt-in-America.pdf : accessed 3 Feb 2015), p. 3.

- Highest Interest Rate—Debts are ordered from highest to smallest interest rate. The interest rate can be found on the monthly statement from your creditor (i.e., credit card or bank). Debts are paid off in this order to minimize interest fees and total amount paid.
- Priority—Pay off debts in order of your priority. This may happen if you have a vested interest in paying off a personal loan from a friend prior to paying the loan from a store or bank.

Example:
Using Debt Snowball, Highest Interest Rate, and Priority Debt Paydown examples:

Current Debt Profile

	Balance	Interest	Monthly Payment
Car Loan	$541,446	4.75%	$140.09
Private Student Loan	$1,725.98	5.00%	$197.91
Macy's Credit Card	$2.00	0	$25.00
Bank of America Credit Card	$675.00	16.24%	$25.00
Introductory Credit Card	$633.37	0.00%	$73.00
Private Vacation Loan	$2,676.94	12.50%	$142.57
Federal Student Loan	$29,157.00	0	$0.00
Total Debt Payments			**$603.57**
Net Income to Pay off Debt			**$300.00**
Total Paid Towards Debt Monthly (Minimum Payments + Net Income)			**$903.57**

Debt Snowball

	Month 1	Month 2	Month 3	Month 4	Month 5	Month 6	Month 7	Month 8
Car Loan	$140.09	$140.09	$140.09	$140.09	$140.09	$140.09	$140.09	$140.09
Private Student Loan	$197.91	$197.91	$197.91	$197.91	$197.91	$197.91	$197.91	$197.91
Macy's Credit Card	$2.00	$0.00	$0.00	$0.00	$0.00	$0.00	$0.00	$0.00
Bank of America Credit Card	$25 + NI ($300) = $325	$25 + NI ($300) = $325	$0	$0	$0	$0	$0	$0
Introductory Credit Card	$73.00	$73.00	$73 + NI = $389	$73 + NI = $389	$0.00	$0.00	$0.00	$0.00
Private Vacation Loan	$142.57	$142.57	$142.57	$142.57	$142.57 + NI = $531.57	$142.57 + NI = $531.57	$142.57 + NI = $531.57	$142.57 + NI = $531.57
Federal Student Loan	$0.00	$0.00	$0.00	$0.00	$0.00	$0.00	$0.00	$0.00

Highest Interest Rate

	Month 1	Month 2	Month 3	Month 4	Month 5	Month 6	Month 7	Month 8
Car Loan	$140.09	$140.09	$140.09	$140.09	$140.09	$140.09	$140.09	$140.09
Private Student Loan	$197.91	$197.91	$197.91	$197.91	$197.91	$197.91	$197.91	$197.91 +NI ($467.57) = $665.48
Macy's Credit Card	$2.00	$0.00	$0.00	$0.00	$0.00	$0.00	$0.00	$0.00
Bank of America Credit Card	$25 + NI ($300) = $325	$25 + NI ($300) = $325	$0	$0	$0	$0	$0	$0
Introductory Credit Card	$73.00	$73.00	$73.00	$73.00	$73.00	$73.00	$73.00	$73.00
Private Vacation Loan	$142.57	$142.57	$142.57 +NI ($325) = $442.57	$142.57 + NI ($325) = $442.57	$142.57 + NI ($325) = $442.57	$142.57 + NI ($325) = $442.57	$142.57 + NI ($325) = $442.57	$0.00
Federal Student Loan	$0.00	$0.00	$0.00	$0.00	$0.00	$0.00	$0.00	$0.00

Priority Debt Pay Off
1) Introductory Credit Card; 2) Car Loan

	Month 1	Month 2	Month 3	Month 4	Month 5	Month 6	Month 7	Month 8
Car Loan	$140.09	$140.09	$140.09 + NI ($373) = $513.09	$140.09 + NI ($373) = $513.09	$140.09 + NI ($373) = $513.09	$140.09 + NI ($373) = $513.09	$140.09 + NI ($373) = $513.09	$140.09 + NI ($373) = $513.09
Private Student Loan	$197.91	$197.91	$197.91	$197.91	$197.91	$197.91	$197.91	$197.91
Macy's Credit Card	$2.00	$0.00	$0.00	$0.00	$0.00	$0.00	$0.00	$0.00
Bank of America Credit Card	$25	$25	$25	$25	$25	$25	$25	$25
Introductory Credit Card	$73 + NI ($300) = $373	$73 + NI ($300) = $373	$0.00	$0.00	$0.00	$0.00	$0.00	$0.00
Private Vacation Loan	$142.57	$142.57	$142.57	$142.57	$142.57	$142.57	$142.57	$142.57
Federal Student Loan	$0.00	$0.00	$0.00	$0.00	$0.00	$0.00	$0.00	$0.00

For a blank debt payoff sheet, go to www.goaldiggersclub.com/membership-homepage/budgeting-resources/ and click "Book Debt Payoff.xls"

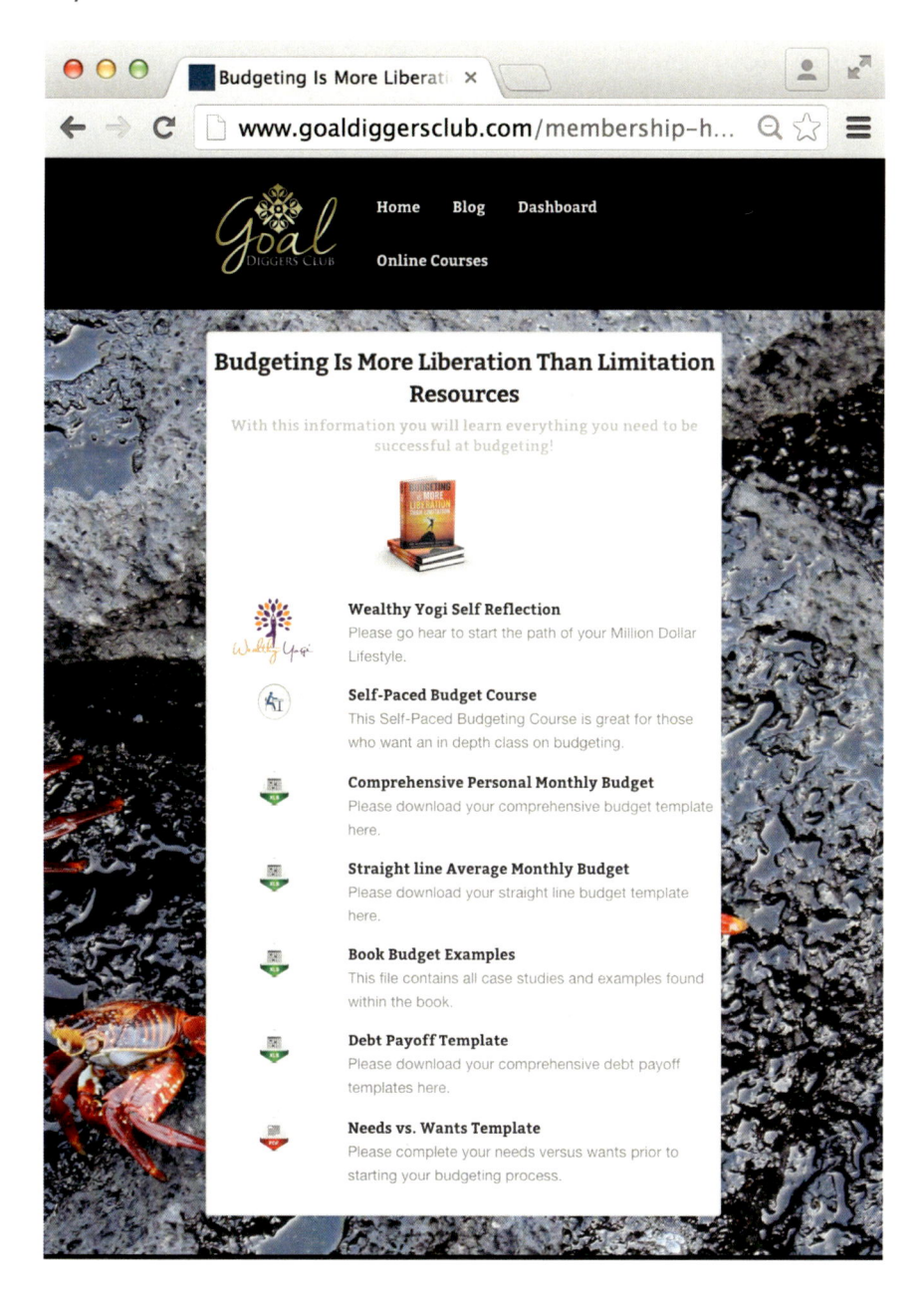

chapter 5: hands-on budget planning

63

It can take years to get out of debt, but the longer you wait to start the further away financial freedom will be.

STEP 5: COMPLETE YOUR EMERGENCY FUND

Your Emergency Fund is money set aside for the worst possible situation. Unfortunately, many people don't have much of an emergency fund to cushion them when inevitable costly circumstances arise.

A 2014 Bankrate.com report indicated that one quarter (26%) of Americans have no emergency savings.[3] Of those who do have savings, only 40 percent have at least three months' worth of expenses saved, and less than half (46%) have six months' worth of expenses saved.

When you begin budgeting regularly, you should start out aiming to save one month's worth of living expenses then work your way to saving three to six months. If you are trying to pay off debt, you should still have an emergency fund to cover one month's worth of expenses. If you use the savings in your emergency fund, replace it as soon as possible.

Now that you know the process, review the case study of Jen and Mike. Answer the questions, then go through the 5-step process for yourself.

CASE STUDY 3: JEN AND MIKE

Here is a case study of hands-on budget planning using Jen and Mike as examples.

---

[3] Bankrate.com, "Financial Security Index: Saving for a rainy day," (http://www.bankrate.com/finance/consumer-index/saving-for-a-rainy-day.aspx: accessed 2 Feb 2015).

Jen is 30 years old and living in Atlanta. She moved there for a job in 2004 with her husband Mike. She makes $65,000 a year; he makes $50,000. They own a 3-bedroom house in the Cabbagetown neighborhood with a 15-year mortgage. Even though they consider themselves successful in their careers and personal achievements, Jen and Mike have no clue where their money goes. They want to make some changes in their lives and they realize they need a budget. Here's where they begin:

Goals:
1. Have a child within the next year;
2. Get a life insurance policy for both;
3. Develop a retirement plan.

Monthly income (after taxes and retirement contributions): $7,000
Total expenses: $7,300
Credit card debt: $15,000
Student loans: $50,000

STEP 1: TRACK AND OBSERVE

Jen and Mike create a budget based on their expenses over the last three months. Their total budget is as follows:

Jen and Mike Initial Straight-Line Budget

Average Monthly Income	
	Total
Jen's After-Tax Income	$4,000
Mike's After-Tax Income	$3,000
Total	**$7,000**
Average Monthly Expenses	
Housing	$1,800
Transportation	$800
Insurance	$150
Food	$450
Pets	$0
Personal Care	$900
Entertainment	$1,200
Credit Cards + Personal Loans	$1,300
Education & Personal Development	$0
Taxes	$0
Savings & Investments	$500
Gifts and Donations	$200
Legal Expense	$0
Total	**$7,300**
Average Net Income Goals	
Net Income	($300)
(Total Income - Total Expenses)	
	Total
Debt	$0
Savings	$0
Other	$0
Applied Net Income	$0

Carefully review Jen and Mike's budget and answer the following questions:

- What problems do you see with their budget?
- What changes would you make and why?

Make your modifications in the "Adjusted Totals" column in the table below:

Average Monthly Income		
	Total	**Adjusted Totals**
Jen's After-Tax Income	$4,000	
Mike's After-Tax Income	$3,000	
Total	**$7,000**	
Average Monthly Expenses		
	Total	**Adjusted Totals**
Housing	$1,800	
Transportation	$800	
Insurance	$150	
Food	$450	
Pets	$0	
Personal Care	$900	
Entertainment	$1,200	
Credit Cards + Personal Loans	$1,300	
Education & Personal Development	$0	
Taxes	$0	
Savings & Investments	$500	
Gifts and Donations	$200	
Legal Expense	$0	
Total	**$7,300**	
Average Net Income Goals		
Net Income (Total Income - Total Expenses)	($300)	
	Total	**Adjusted Totals**
Debt	$0	
Savings	$0	
Other	$0	
Applied Net Income	$0	

chapter 5: hands-on budget planning

STEP 2: BUDGETING MAKEOVER

At this rate, Jen and Mike are getting deeper into debt every month, so they need to makeover their budget. They realize they need to make some changes. The most logical first step is to spend less than they make. By spending less than they make, they can achieve some of their financial goals.

They can save $100 on utilities by fixing a leaky faucet, weather proofing all the windows and doors, and programming their thermostat. They decide to switch Internet providers and lock down a low gas rate. They plan to give up their gym memberships and start a free fitness group that meets at the park twice a week. They also plan to give up memberships in social clubs with fees. They commit to cutting out half their entertainment budget. Instead of driving separately and paying for two parking passes, Jen will drop Mike off at work, saving them $70 a month. They will also run errands together to save on gas for a total savings of $30.

They have found out their lifestyles were not reflective of their finances or their goals. They have discovered alternative options that fit their finances and personalities. For instance, they plan to host a monthly movie night with friends they used to eat out with, and Jen decides to start a book club to interact with friends regularly.

After cutting out many luxuries they once considered necessities, such as a cleaning service, smart phones, shopping trips, cable TV, and various social clubs, Jen and Mike have made the commitment to follow these rules to make sure they stay on target with their budget.

The next step they take is to earn more. Jen decides to dog sit and to start writing freelance for local news blogs. Mike decides to take on clients for personal fitness training sessions. If Mike finds three fitness clients and Jen has four 3-day weekend pet jobs and files five freelance articles a month, this will add $700 from Mike plus $300 from Jen. Their total additional monthly income will be $1,000.

Even though their new budget gives them a gain of $1100 every month, they still need term life insurance, estate planning, and a savings fund for their impending pregnancy.

The changes Jen and Mike make are reflected in their budget below:

Average Monthly Income	
	Total
Jen's After-Tax Income	$4,000
Mike's After-Tax Income	$3,000
Jen's Dog Sitting Income	$300
Mike's Personal Training Income	$700
Total	**$8,000**
Average Monthly Expenses	
	Total
Housing	$1,700
Transportation	$700
Insurance	$150
Food	$450
Pets	$0
Personal Care	$700
Entertainment	$1,200
Credit Cards + Personal Loans	$1,300
Education & Personal Development	$0
Taxes	$0
Savings & Investments	$500
Gifts and Donations	$200
Legal Expense	$0
Total	**$6,900**

chapter 5: hands-on budget planning

Average Net Income Goals	
Net Income (Total Income - Total Expenses)	$1,100
	Total
Debt	$0
Savings	$0
Other	$0
Applied Net Income	$0

Once they are able to increase their net income and adjust their expenses, they can move on to the next step of the planning process.

STEP 3: START AN EMERGENCY FUND

Since Jen and Mike have never had a budget, they didn't know what an emergency fund was until they had to scramble to fix the plumbing in their newly-purchased—but very old—house and suddenly wished they had the money saved so they could pay cash. Instead, they charged $15,000 worth of home improvement projects to their credit card.

To avoid getting into the same situation again, Jen and Mike decide to save 5 percent of their monthly income in a separate savings account. They agree not to use the money for anything except emergencies, which they have defined as household repairs, medical expenses not covered by insurance, and unexpected auto repairs. By not using the money to pay for their wants, their emergency fund will increase and provide them with a comfortable financial cushion.

STEP 4: DEBT PAY DOWN

One of Jen and Mike's goals is to have a baby next year, but they don't want any debt hanging over their heads. They decide to use a portion of their increased net income to pay off their $15,000 credit card debt. To keep the credit cards paid off, they agree not to use credit card debt or indulge in other bad habits that do not align with their priorities.

STEP 5: COMPLETE EMERGENCY FUND

Jen and Mike estimate the new baby they plan to have will increase their monthly expenses by $500. As such, they decide to add six months of expenses to their emergency fund in order to complete the fund. The additional money for the emergency fund will come from the increased net income.

RESULT

At the end of each month, Jen and Mike had a shortfall of $300, which accumulated each month. They did not realize that their credit card shuffle was digging them deeper and deeper into debt.

Once they developed a budget and a plan to achieve their goals, they tracked their expenses for three months, created a realistic budget, made adjustments, and arrived at a result. Jen and Mike were shocked by where their money went each month. Like them, you should track your spending and then list your financial priorities.

ASSIGNMENT:

Now it's your turn to complete your budget.

Like Jen and Mike, you have certain financial goals. Complete this assignment based on your experience, reviewing Jen and Mike's goals and budget.

Download a blank Straight-Line Budget worksheet at www.goaldiggersclub.com/membership-homepage/budgeting-resources/.

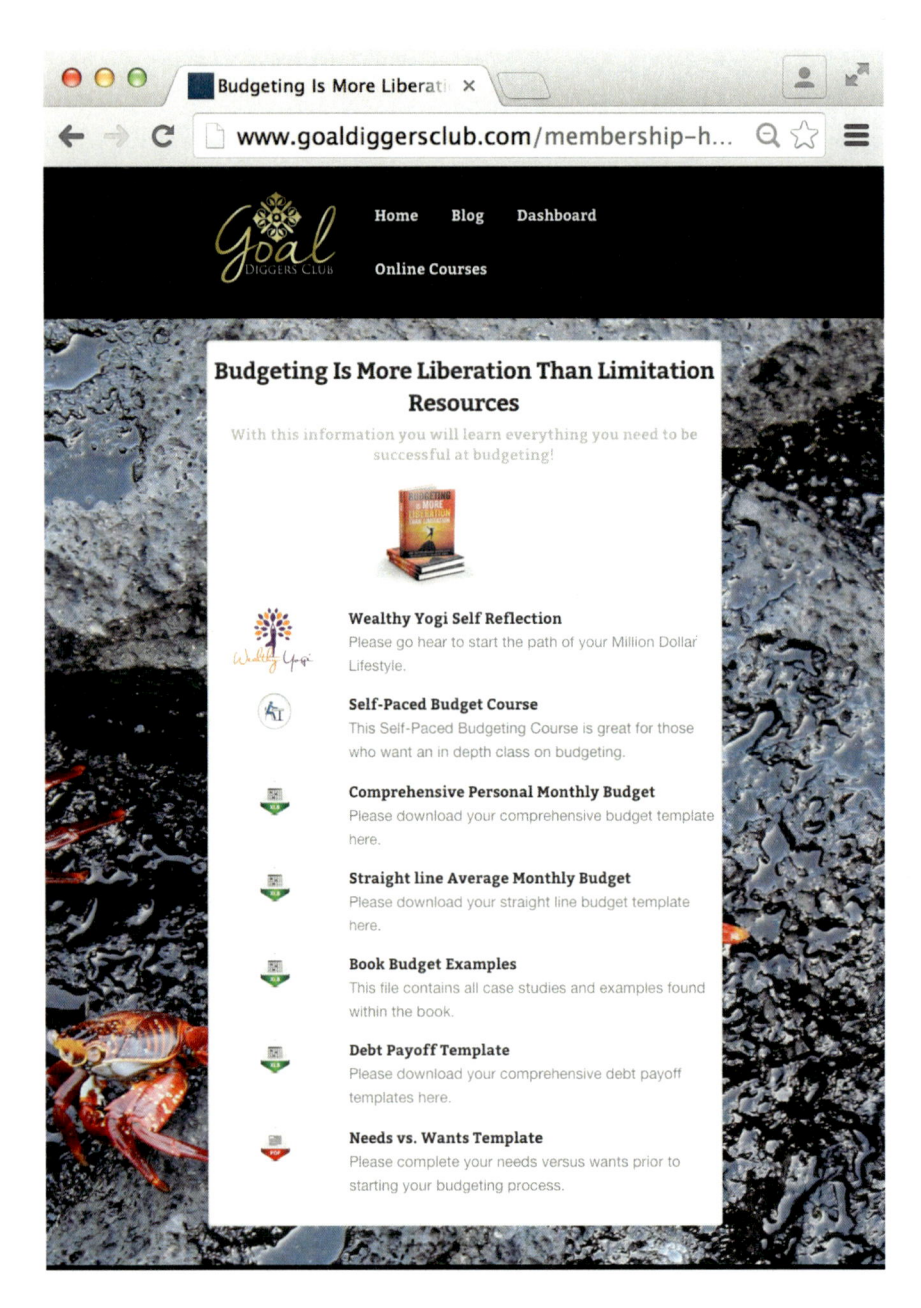

- For a blank debt payoff sheet, click on "Straight Line Average Monthly Budget.xls".
- Write down one financial goal you have.
- In the budget worksheet, insert your monthly totals.
- What changes can you make to improve your financial situation and achieve your stated goal?
- Explain your justifications for your changes.
- Use a new chart and make your modifications to indicate the adjustments.

Be sure your budget is reasonable and feasible. You need to be able to stick to the plan to be successful. Otherwise, you will not be able to reach your goals.

Your budget should show you where you can cut back in certain areas, such as gasoline costs (by limiting long-distance driving and exploring your own neighborhood instead); buying only the clothing you need and will wear (instead of hoarding in hopes of wearing items later); or cooking more meals at home (instead of eating out at costly restaurants multiple times per week).

Some immediate ways to change your budget are:
- Negotiate with creditors;
- Negotiate utility costs;
- Look into debt consolidation;
- Reduce interest rates;
- Save to buy.

ROAD TO WEALTH CHALLENGE

Once you have become proficient with creating, adjusting, and sticking to your budget, you can shift your focus to wealth creation. To help get you in the mindset of living a wealthy lifestyle, use the 5-Week Road to Wealth Challenge that can be found at www.WealthChallenges.com.

In this 5-week challenge, you will assess your life and determine the goals you would like to reach in order to live your ideal lifestyle. By the end of the 5 weeks, you should have a picture of your ideal million-dollar lifestyle and a completed long-term million-dollar lifestyle plan. You will be equipped to complete more advanced wealth challenges and put your life on the fast track for success.

Be sure to join the online community at www.goaldiggersclub.com/ to share your challenges and successes.

FINAL THOUGHT

Budget planning is essential to finding financial liberation. The level of planning should be as detailed as is feasible and useful for your life and situation. You should update your budget whenever there is a change in your life status, income, or desired pathway. Also, your budget should serve as a mirror for your life's goals and priorities. If you've always dreamed of buying a field and starting your own farm, that should be factored into your budget. Don't spend so much time focusing on your daily responsibilities that you forget about your dreams.

CHAPTER 6: WISE HABITS

"We are what we repeatedly do. Excellence, therefore, is not an act but a habit."
— Aristotle

The slow and steady way to accomplishing most things in life is through your habits. This idea also holds true with your financial budgeting actions. Wise financial habits can be boiled down to simple steps you can complete no matter your income level.

THINK BEFORE YOU SPEND

You must get into the habit of spending money based on your budgeted requirements, not based on whether or not you have the money on hand. This takes discipline, and discipline is necessary when budgeting.

It is not the big purchases you need to keep an eye on; it is the small ones. Imagine spending $5 here and $10 there every few days. You could find yourself spending $100 a month or more on things that don't support the lifestyle you want and don't support your budget. Before you buy that specialty coffee, consider whether that one purchase will prevent you from being able to take the ski trip you've budgeted for.

Depriving yourself of the little things is not the point; creating and executing a plan so you can comfortably enjoy the little things while pursuing the larger things is the point.

> **Not knowing how much you spend is the first budgeting mistake.**

Think of it as conscious spending. You are the best judge of how to spend or save your money in order to improve the quality of your life. Financial planning aids in evaluating every purchase. Is buying the gym membership right now extravagant? Is buying a laptop at this time in your career a necessity?

Retail therapy feels great, but buyer's remorse does not. Knowing how much money you have to work with and thinking about the consequences of investing those monies in certain products or services help you budget for the things that truly matter to you in the long run. Consider the pros and cons of every purchase, and become more aware of your buying habits. Being able to afford everything would be great, but if you are not in a financial position to do so, take into account what matters to you, and make an active effort to only spend on what gives you the maximum satisfaction of knowing what your money has gone toward.

Money management is a simple yet powerful tool you can master by practicing it regularly. Once money management becomes a habit, you will automatically adjust to real-world financial changes without much stress. You will be protected in case of emergencies, and you will be able to plan a way out of any situation.

KEEP TRACK OF YOUR EXPENSES

Use your bank statements to keep up with your expenses. If you usually use cash, make a special point to use your debit card to track your purchases. The debit card gives you a statement to show how and where you are spending your cash.

Mint.com is a great tool for tracking expenses. It helps you categorize your expenses so you will know how much you are spending and on what. Not knowing how much you spend is the first budgeting mistake. You can't improve your financial situation if you don't know what it is, what your habits are, and how to make adjustments.

Source: Mint.com

Keeping an eye on your expenses is crucial to your financial planning experience. This is your money. You must know, at all times, where it goes and what it gets you. Just like your garden will never grow without you taking the time and effort to water the plants in it, your wealth will not flourish until you invest the time to nurture it.

An important part of tracking your expenses includes ensuring nobody else is using your money. Too often, a familiar looking charge on your credit card goes unnoticed until one day you realize that over a period of six months, that figure has ballooned to more than a few thousand dollars and you never even initiated those transactions!

By tracking your expenses, you can detect a fraudulent charge on your cards right away. Commit to keeping your expenses in check, and embrace the fact that this is an essential part of your path to financial wellbeing.

SPEND LESS THAN YOU MAKE

This can be much easier said than done. Once you know how much you're spending, adjustments can be made to cut back and ensure that your income exceeds your spending. It's impossible to save and eliminate debt when you spend more than your income allows.

You can improve your financial situation when you compare your expenses and income. This is a simple practice that can improve your financial snapshot. The knowledge you gain from completing this task is a step in the right direction toward financial success.

MINDFUL SPENDING CAN BECOME MINDFUL LIVING

Mindful spending is an essential element of budgeting that helps you live your best life. You might fail to consider where your money is going and why you're sending it in that particular direction.

After taking a snapshot of your finances, you will become aware of where you are spending your income. You cannot overlook the fact that you spent $100 on lunch one week when you're struggling to pay off your student loans.

Practicing mindfulness while doing your daily activities allows you to experience the benefits of a mindful lifestyle.

LIFESTYLE STORY

▼ LIVING IN YOUR DREAM CITY

Yvonne had achieved her ideal work/life balance. In the nonprofit sector, she made great connections that helped ensure she always made her fundraising goals. Although she enjoyed her job and her lifestyle, her dream was to live in a new city. However, she had to figure out how to structure her finances to accomplish her dreams.

She put a strict budget into motion. With little credit card debt and an already low interest rate on her mortgage, she began to save more money than ever before. Instead of her weekly girls' night out parties, she cut the outings to monthly, saving nearly $250 a month. She did this until she saved enough to pay for moving expenses. She also decided to sell her car to have an additional cushion to pay for moving incidentals. Once this plan was in motion, she moved on to Phase 2.

She started setting up informational interviews at nonprofits in Portland, Oregon, so when an opening came up they would think of her. About a year later, a job opened in Portland. She had just been awarded a huge promotion at her job in Houston and was torn about taking a step down to follow her dream to move to Portland. However, after two years of putting her dream in motion, she took the leap and achieved the life she desired.

chapter 6: wise habits

FINAL THOUGHT

A habit is created when you do the same thing consistently and frequently over time. The same is true about the role of finances in your life. Tasks that at first seem burdensome or boring end up being routine. You'll increase efficiency by reviewing and perfecting your budget over time. In fact, you'll start shaping your financial instincts to the point where you may not need to review your budget as often because your purchasing decisions will be in line with your dreams, goals, and finances.

PART THREE: TO LIBERATE, NOT LIMIT

> *"Money is only a tool. It will take you wherever you wish, but it will not replace you as the driver."*
> *— Ayn Rand*

Money is a powerful tool that allows you to have the experiences and tangible items you want and need to enjoy your life, to be able to help others, and to build a secure future. This tool can be used to create or destroy; therefore, you should learn to use it responsibly, and budgeting is the best way to do so.

As you've learned through the examples in this book, budgeting is a source of liberation, not limitation. Your budget frees you from worrying about how much money you have, questioning whether you can afford to buy something, and being afraid you'll never be able to fund the lifestyle of your dreams.

When you practice the simple concepts in this book you will understand that the only financial limitations placed on you are those you have placed on yourself. There is nothing you cannot have or experience when you liberate yourself from the limiting thoughts and behaviors of the past and begin to consistently practice responsible budget planning and financial management strategies.

Are you ready to be liberated?

CHAPTER 7: EVERY DOLLAR MATTERS

*"A budget is telling your money where to go
instead of wondering where it went."*
– Dave Ramsey

D o not be deceived; everything matters, down to the last cent. Life cannot be compartmentalized; everything works together. Eating at your favorite restaurant instead of eating the leftovers at home matters. What matters is not just the extra $5. What matters is that the extra money spent is the same money you aren't using to pay down your credit card balance, which then results in:

1. a higher principal;
2. higher interest accumulation;
3. longer payoff periods.

All of this results in less money to accomplish your goals and to experience your dreams, whether that means taking a vacation or supporting your favorite charity. Granted, what you want to do with the extra money could very well be to go to the restaurant, but you need to be certain that whatever you decide to spend your hard-earned money on is significant to you.

SUCCESS IS IN THE DETAILS

CASE STUDY 4: LUNCH

Brian has a unique ordering style when he goes to his favorite lunch spot. He orders the chicken burrito off the lunch menu and asks for extra chicken. His companion Andre orders the dinner portion. Their plates are mostly indistinguishable, but their checks are not.

Brian has budgeted for this expense, is counting his pennies, and knows what value he should receive for the money he spends. But can the same be said about Andre?

> **MENU**
>
> Brian's Lunch price = $14.90
> $12.95 with choice of soup or salad
> $1.95 for extra chicken
>
> Andre's Dinner Price = $16.95
> $16.95 without soup or salad

Where did the difference in the total amounts of their checks occur? In some cases, the difference is simply a loophole that may eventually get plugged when the restaurant or client figures it out. In other cases, this price difference is something that businesses don't expect the consumer to notice and can, therefore, be turned into a profit for the business if customers don't realize they're actually paying more. The point is: every dollar matters, so all money should be accounted for.

CASE STUDY 5: DIAPERS

Cory buys diapers in bulk to limit his number of trips to the store, expecting a better per-diaper price at the big-box store. However, this might not always be correct. Sometimes the price difference between the bulk diapers and the smaller package is due to a sale or markdown, and other times there really is no price difference at all. The store is simply taking advantage of Cory's (and other customers') assumptions that there is a deal on bulk items.

Imagine that a fair price per diaper is about $0.13. Cory purchases the ultra large bulk package of 300 diapers for $54 at the big-box store, making his per-diaper cost $0.18. If he had purchased the smaller package of 100 diapers for $14 at the local drug store he would have paid only $0.14 per diaper. He could have purchased three of the 100-count packages (300 diapers) for only $42; a $12 saving.

Cory could have easily used the calculator on his cell phone to do the math and figure out if he was getting a deal or getting ripped off at the big-box store.

CASE STUDY 6: SODA

Jessica enjoys having an ice-cold soda each afternoon at work. Soda from the snack machine costs $1 per can. If she took the time to think about it, she'd realize she's spending $5 per week or $20 per month on soda. Over a 3-month period, that's $60, or $240 per year!

Considering that Jessica wants to save for a weekend getaway at a nearby resort, she's actually drinking away her getaway money day by day. Remember, every dollar matters.

FUND YOUR PASSIONATE PURSUITS

Creating a budget isn't just about paying off debt or taking care of bills. Your budget allows you to live the life of your dreams right now. Rather than just telling yourself you're going to save for those luxuries or experiences, actually do it and put your dreams in your budget.

You might have the urge to explore the world. That wanderlust often leaves you planning vacations to interesting and exotic locales as often as possible. For example, Susan enjoys travel and might take several trips a year, from local hideaways to international locations. One of the line items on her budget is "travel." She consistently sets aside money to do what she loves. Some months that amount is only $50 while other months she is able to set aside $200. Over time, this habit has enabled her to pursue most of her passions.

Your life won't always take the path you outline, no matter how meticulously you plan. Audrey is an accountant who has a beautiful vegetable garden at her home and she loves to share her bounty with friends and family. At the suggestion of a close friend, she decided to volunteer at a local farm. Two years later, she is no longer an accountant and now works full time on the farm. She was able to make such a drastic change due to strict financial planning.

The income generated by a new farmer is much less than that of a seasoned accountant, but by cutting unnecessary expenses and crafting a budget in preparation of her reduced income, Audrey made the change and accomplished her goal.

Consider Karen, a high-ranking corporate executive who works with AmeriCorps. Although the spirit of service and giving is important to her, the trappings of corporate America are enticing. By reworking her expenses and putting them into a service fund, she spends vacations giving back while maintaining the lifestyle corporate America affords her.

Often your dreams look completely different from your reality. You might pursue careers based on areas in which you excel rather than the passions that fill your heart. But as you age, those career pursuits might leave you unfulfilled. By then, you could be financially beholden to a company or commitment you don't love, and might find yourself spending hours each day wondering if you'll ever get out. The first step to making that change can be creating a budget that reflects your true dreams.

Perhaps your dream is to live in Las Vegas for a year and become a lounge singer. If you're an elementary school teacher this may seem a far-off goal, unattainable based on your current income and responsibilities. However, after meeting with a financial planner, mapping out a plan, and being disciplined with your spending, you could find yourself one day flying to Las Vegas to audition to sing at the Bellagio. This change in lifestyle may not happen as quickly for you as it would for someone who is independently wealthy, but it is entirely possible and reasonable to pursue.

Even if your dreams are more traditional, such as building your dream home and having a family, you must plan to ensure those dreams are realized. All goals require planning, organization, and dedication to be reached.

Asya is a stay-at-home mom who loves to teach, but was unable to attend college because of her newborn. Undaunted, she crafted a plan by becoming a part-time babysitter and saving the money. This plan provided a steady playmate for her daughter, allowing Asya to start college when her daughter entered Pre-K. Although the returns took a few years, the planning and budgeting paid off in multiple ways. Asya created a situation where her daughter developed a strong bond with another child early in her childhood, and Asya was able to finance her own education.

Like most people, you desire a life of happiness and contentment. You can have this when balance exists and when you are in control of your personal path. Since all decisions are connected, your priorities, values, perceptions, habits, and circumstances all impact the usefulness and results of your budget.

FINAL THOUGHT

Budgeting is a financial undertaking, but it can and will impact other areas of your life. You will learn many life lessons as you go through the process of crafting a budget. By taking control of your finances, you open your mind to the reality of taking control of your life. Use the tools and case studies in this chapter to make sure your budget is useful and appropriate for your life.

CHAPTER 8: CONTINUE TO CONQUER

"Self-respect is the root of discipline. The sense of dignity grows with the ability to say no to oneself."
– Abraham Joshua Heschel

Life should be lived in the present. Now is the time that counts, but throwing caution and reason to the wind to enjoy this life is unnecessary. You now have a practical tool you can use to create the life you want without risking the life you've built.

> **Create the life you want without risking the life you've built.**

You are probably familiar with experiencing financial fear or limitation from time to time. Many fear unemployment, unplanned catastrophes, health issues, transportation problems, and issues with their home. Although you cannot prevent anything bad from happening, you can be prepared for these situations if you have a budget. A budget can provide a cushion for emergency situations, which will reduce the stress and anxiety when the unexpected happens. Maintain perspective on your financial goals, and conquer any limiting fears that creep up.

Throughout your life you will learn that reality does not always fall in line with your plans, and that is all right. When that happens, you now have the tools to conquer your financial obstacles and calibrate your life so you can get back on track.

Your goals and dreams may differ from someone else's, but the process to accomplish them is the same. Every dollar you spend or don't spend counts toward your goals. By becoming aware of where your dollars go you are taking control of your finances and can freely expand your life in a way that is aligned with your desires.

Budgeting isn't about counting each penny, but rather understanding that your dollars need to be accounted for, and using them with intention.

Budgeting isn't about limitation. Budgeting is a tool of liberation and empowerment. A budget allows you to use money to support your life's purpose. By keeping track of your finances, you can live your best life unencumbered by the stress that can come when you don't feel you have control of your financial future.

You can't know for certain what the outcome of your life will be, but you can imagine—and plan for—what you want it to be.

THANK YOU

Thank you for your interest in seeing how your budget can help guide your path to true freedom. Be the example of budgeting and freedom in action so others will know, by your lifestyle, that budgeting truly is liberating!

All the best,
Roshawnna

ABOUT THE AUTHORS

Roshawnna and Roosevelt are financial practitioners and educators who help others obtain financial self-awareness and knowledge. Born in San Diego, CA, they learned to appreciate money management at a young age under the guidance of their mother.

They both enjoy outdoor activities and spending time with loved ones. Roshawnna founded Novellus Financial in order to provide worry-free solutions to those who feel lost when it comes to financial wellness. To learn more, visit www.novellusfinancial.com.

ROSHAWNNA NOVELLUS, D.SC.

"I hope you live a life you're proud of. If you find that you're not, I hope you find the strength to start all over again."
– Eric Roth,
The Curious Case of Benjamin Button

Everyone has problems and roadblocks that may be real or imaginary. Roshawnna's clients know that they have someone in their corner who will help them get back on track and remind them of their goals. By nurturing and providing support to goal-oriented people, she helps others live their ideal life. Starting Novellus Financial to help people achieve their goals and go after their dreams was a natural step for her.

Roshawnna's passion for teaching financial literacy evolved while volunteering for the IRS Volunteer Income Tax Assistance Program (VITA) in 2011 and 2012. This gave her the platform to provide free tax advice and preparation to low-income taxpayers. After this opportunity, she taught community financial empowerment seminars for families to educate them about their financial options.

Proud Financial Accomplishment: Roshawnna's first major financial goal was to get through college debt-free. She worked as hard as possible to receive the highest grades in high school, then applied for over 200 scholarships to ensure she reached that goal. All that hard work paid off when she was awarded over $600,000 in scholarships and fellowships that paid for all four of her higher education degrees.

Next Financial Goal: Paying off her mortgage and taking her family on international trips.

Roshawnna holds a Doctor of Science in systems engineering, with a minor in finance from George Washington University, a Master of Science in information technology emphasizing information systems engineering, a Bachelor of Arts in business management economics, and a Bachelor of Science in computer engineering, achieving Summa Cum Laude in each.

She is federally licensed as an Enrolled Agent to represent taxpayers in front of the IRS, and also has passed the Series 7 Exam. She is a member of the National Association of Tax Professionals and National Association of Enrolled Agents, and has attended the National Tax Practice Institute.

Roshawnna has created the Goal Diggers Club, a community of goal-driven people who accomplish their goals by making smart financial decisions. Join the Goal Diggers Club to connect with this support system as you pursue your goals: www.goaldiggersclub.com. Read about what Roshawnna learned in Thailand while reaching her goal of being a certified yoga instructor: http://www.goaldiggersclub.com/series/thailand-yoga-mini-retirement

Connect With Roshawnna:
LinkedIn: http://www.linkedin.com/in/roshawnna
Twitter: https://twitter.com/drnovellus
Instagram: http://instagram.com/wealthyyogi

Financial Website: http://www.novellusfinancial.com
Financial Blog: http://novellusfinancialnews.com
Personal Website: http://www.thewealthyyogi.com
Goal Diggers Club Membership Site: http://www.goaldiggersclub.com
YouTube: http://www.youtube.com/user/NovellusFinancial
Amazon: http://amazon.com/author/roshawnnanovellus

ROOSEVELT J. SCALES

"Life does not consist in the abundance of our possessions; it resides in the midst of contentment and virtue." – Luke 12:15

Roosevelt believes that the best things in life are free, but also that nothing is truly free. Therefore, his desire is to promote the value of financial planning.

Regardless of net worth or future aspirations, planning increases the likelihood of turning opportunities into successes. Planning takes discipline, which isn't about denying yourself, but about cultivating the ability to assert your will over circumstances. Financial planning isn't just about wealth accumulation, home purchases, and retirement. Financial planning is about financing your desires, whatever they may be.

Roosevelt's experience is in corporate accounting and finance. Still, he most values his life application skills. His passion is to help free people from the constraints they are subject to through questioning and evaluating everything in their lives, and ultimately, developing a plan.

Proud Financial Accomplishment: Roosevelt's greatest joy is providing his two children the opportunity to have their mother available to raise and care for them without the necessity of her working.

Next Financial Goal: To become debt free.

Roosevelt has an MBA in finance and a Bachelor's degree in management information systems.

WHAT'S NEXT?

We are happy to help you in your quest to maintain a reasonable and feasible budget. We offer a free self-paced online budgeting course with exercises and worksheets.

To access the course, visit www.goaldiggersclub.com/membership-homepage/budgeting-resources/ and click on "Self-Paced Budget Course."

RESOURCES

All resources, examples, and exercises listed in this book are located at www.goaldiggersclub.com/budgeting-resources/

1. Novellus Financial: Offers several budgeting and planning resources. www.novellusfinancial.com
2. Novellus Financial Blog: Contains a variety of articles on how to improve your finances, credit score, and wealth profile. www.novellusfinancialnews.com
3. Goal Diggers Club: A community that supports individuals in reaching their life goals. www.goaldiggersclub.com
4. Forbes.com: Offers articles reviewing budgeting software and phone applications. Search for "budgeting software options" at www.forbes.com
5. About.com: Provides a list and in-depth analysis of budgeting tools and resources. http://financialsoft.about.com/od/budgetingsoftware/tp/Envelope_Budget_Software.htm
6. LevelMoney.com: Offers an innovative way to track your budget on the go. https://levelmoney.com
7. Mint.com: Offers a free way to securely link all financial accounts, provide alerts, tracking, forecasting, and automated budgeting. www.mint.com
8. LearnVest.com: Pairs all its users with someone to guide them on their financial journey. This is a great service for those who need a little extra help. www.learnvest.com
9. BudgetEase.com: Offers alternative budgeting software for those who do not like the experience of Mint. It is a great resource for those who want a full online budgeting option. www.budgetease.com
10. The Nest: Offers The Nest's Budgeting section, a handy aid for

all types of specific budgeting needs. http://budgeting.thenest.com/

11. Dave Ramsey: Offers a suite of budgeting tools and templates. www.daveramsey.com/tools/budget-forms/

12. Kiplinger: Features an online budgeting tool that lets you obtain a quick budget. www.kiplinger.com/tool/spending/T007-S001-budgeting-worksheet-a-household-budget-for-today-a/

13. Some of the paid apps you can find with better usability and added tools include: Moneywiz, Dollarbird, Spendee, and Home-Budget with Sync.